Beginner Family Bible Study

10 Minute Daily Devotional For Families To Deepen Their Faith

John Bernthal

©2015

© Copyright 2015 by John Bernthal - All rights reserved.

This document is geared towards providing exact and reliable information in regards to the topic and issue covered. The publication is sold with the idea that the publisher is not required to render accounting, officially permitted, or otherwise, qualified services. If advice is necessary, legal or professional, a practiced individual in the profession should be ordered.

- From a Declaration of Principles which was accepted and approved equally by a Committee of the American Bar Association and a Committee of Publishers and Associations.

In no way is it legal to reproduce, duplicate, or transmit any part of this document in either electronic means or in printed format. Recording of this publication is strictly prohibited and any storage of this document is not allowed unless with written permission from the publisher. All rights reserved.

The information provided herein is stated to be truthful and consistent, in that any liability, in terms of inattention or otherwise, by any usage or abuse of any policies, processes, or directions contained within is the solitary and utter responsibility of the recipient reader. Under no circumstances will any legal responsibility or blame be held against the publisher for any reparation, damages, or monetary loss due to the information herein, either directly or indirectly.

Respective authors own all copyrights not held by the publisher.

The information herein is offered for informational purposes solely, and is universal as so. The presentation of the information is without contract or any type of guarantee assurance.

The trademarks that are used are without any consent, and the publication of the trademark is without permission or backing by the trademark owner. All trademarks and brands within this book are for clarifying purposes only and are the owned by the owners themselves, not affiliated with this document.

Introduction

Prayer #1: Forgiveness

Prayer #2: Alertness

Prayer #3: Contentment

Prayer #4: Material Possessions, aka Stuff

Prayer #5: Obedience

Prayer #6: Missions

Prayer #7: Dependability

Prayer #8: Faith

Prayer #9: Bullying

Prayer #10: Creativity

Prayer #11: Hospitality

Prayer #12: Kindness

Prayer #13: Making decisions

Prayer #14: Love

Prayer #15: Humility

Prayer #16: Serving God

Prayer #17: Worship

Prayer #18: Listening to you

Prayer #19: Knowing the Bible

Prayer #20 Trust

Prayer #21: Thankfulness

Prayer #22: Truth

Prayer #23: Anger

Prayer #24: Grief

Prayer #25: Health and Safety

Prayer #26: Right vs. Wrong

Prayer #27: Our world

Prayer #28: Joy

Prayer #29: Patience

Prayer #30: Sensitivity

Introduction

While there is some truth to the old saying, 'actions speak louder than words', words have a tremendous power to heal, to hurt, to build up, to tear down, and to convey our thoughts and feelings when nothing else can get the job done. Think about it...if God didn't intend for us to communicate through words, we wouldn't need ears or voices. We also wouldn't have made the advancement from silent movies to 'talkies' (as they were called) or had a need to invent the telephone (ones we actually spoke through rather than texted).

Yes, words are powerful, but they are also something we want and desire. We want to hear the words like:

- *Please*

- *Thank you*

- *I love you*

- *I appreciate you*

- *Good job*

- *You are special*

- *I trust you*

- *I need you*

- *I'm sorry*

- *I forgive you*

There are even times when we want to hear words such as:

- *I need you to understand*

- *You hurt me*

- *You can do better*

- *Don't do that*
- *Think before you act or speak*

- *You are wrong*

- *I'm willing to give you another chance*

Not only do we want and need to hear these words, we need to *say* them. We need to say them to our spouses, children, extended family, friends, and most of all, to God the Father through Jesus. In other words, we need to pray these words—and as parents we need to teach our children to pray these words.

When our children are learning to talk we give them simple words to pray; "Thank you Jesus for Daddy, Mommy, our house our food, and for you, Jesus. I love you, Jesus, amen." (at least that's how it went at our house). But as they got older we taught them to make their prayers more personal and relevant to what was going on in their lives. The purpose of this book is to start you on your way to doing the same for your family; making prayer personal and relevant in the lives of each member of your family.

Each of the following prayers touches on a particular subject matter or character trait God desires us to have. Use these prayers as a foundation for going deeper into conversation with Jesus who intercedes on our behalf.

After each prayer you will find questions that are intended to be used as a catalyst for discussion between you and your children and to plant the seeds of desire for a deeper relationship with the LORD. We pray that this book will serve these purposes and result in bringing your family closer together and closer to God.

Prayer #1: Forgiveness

Dear God,

Thank you for being you. Thank you for loving us and for sending Jesus to die on the cross for our sins. God, please forgive me for hurting you by sinning and help me to want to do better.

I know the Bible says you will not forgive us unless we forgive others, so make my heart a forgiving heart. Let me forgive people when they hurt my feelings and aren't kind to me—even if they don't ask me to. And when I am unkind to someone I want you to make my heart and my mind feel sad until I ask that person to forgive me. God, I want to be like you.

In Jesus' name I pray, amen.

Questions:

1. Read Matthew 6:14-15. How does it make you feel to know you must forgive others if you want Jesus to forgive you?

2. Do you need to ask someone to forgive you? If so, will you?

3. Why do you think God needs us to ask his forgiveness if he knows everything we do, how we feel and what we are thinking?

Prayer #2: Alertness

Dear God,

Thank you for loving me and taking such good care of me and my family. Thank you for knowing everything—for knowing what we need even before we do.

God, help me be alert, too. Help me know what I need to do to be like you. Help me understand what I read in the Bible. Help me listen to what you say.

I want you to make my heart, my head, and my eyes alert and aware to what I can do for others, too. Tell me when I need to cheer someone up and what I can do to make them feel better. Tell me when I need to be a better listener. Tell me when I need to share with others. Help me want to tell other people about you because I want others to see Jesus in me so that they can know him, too.

In Jesus' name I pray, amen.

Questions:

1. Read Matthew 25:42-45. What do you think these verses mean?

2. Name five ways God shows you he is watching over you.

3. Name five ways you can show others you are aware of their needs and that you care about them like Jesus does.

Prayer #3: Contentment

Dear God,

Thank you for being so wise and for knowing what I need and for taking such great care of my family and me. Thank you for the house we live in, the food we eat, the clothes we wear, and for the fun things we have to play with and enjoy.

I am asking you, God, to make sure I am always thankful for what I have. Don't let me get greedy and want more and more. Help me be content with what I have. I don't ever want to think that the things I have are more important than you are. I never want to love my things more than I love you, so please protect my heart from feeling this way.

Help me never forget that everything I have comes from you. Help me to always trust you. Make my heart happy because I know you always do what is best for me.

In Jesus' name I pray, amen.

Questions:

1. Read Matthew 6:28-29 and 33. What do you think these verses mean?

2. Why do you think God doesn't always give us what we ask for or what we want?

3. What toy, book, game, or other item is your favorite? How would you feel if you didn't have it anymore?

4. Would you love God less if you didn't have it anymore? Why or why not?

Prayer #4: Material Possessions, aka Stuff

Dear God,

Thank you for the things you give me and my family and thank you for loving us so much that you sent your son, Jesus, to die on the cross for us.

God, thank you for all the nice things you give me; my house, my clothes, my food, my toys, and my pets. Help me take really good care of everything you give me so that I can show you how thankful I am for these things.

I really like all the things you have given me, but God, please help me to not be greedy and to think these things are more important than loving you. Help me be good at sharing my things. Help me be able to give my things to other people who need them more than I do. Help me show others that you are more important than anything else in the world.

In Jesus' name I pray, amen.

Questions:

1. Read Matthew 6:19-21. Why do you think Jesus warns us about loving our stuff too much?

2. What things would it be hard for you to give up? Why?

3. Challenge for every family member: Pick two or three things you really like and give them to someone in need.

Prayer #5: Obedience

Dear God,

Thank you for loving us and for sending Jesus to die on the cross for our sins. Thank you for giving us the Bible so we will know how to obey you so that we can be in heaven with you someday.

God, please give me a heart that wants to obey you—even when it is hard or I don't understand why you want me to do something. Help me obey you by loving everyone and treating other people the way I want them to treat me.

Help me to obey my parents so I don't get in trouble or get hurt. Help me know my parents have rules because they love me. Stop me from getting angry at my parents when they discipline me for breaking the rules.

Help me obey my teachers at school and help me follow the rules when I'm playing a game so that I my friends like to play with me.

Most of all, God, help me obey the Bible by telling other people about you.

In Jesus' name I pray, amen.

Questions:

1. Read Ephesians 6:1-3. Why does God tell us to obey our parents?

2. What rules at your house do you have a hard time obeying? Why?

3. How do you think it makes your parents feel when you disobey?

4. When is it hard for you to obey God? Why?

5. How do you think it makes God fell when you disobey?

Prayer #6: Missions

Dear God,

Thank you for loving us and for giving us the Bible. Thank you for telling your disciples to tell everyone on the world about Jesus and how he died on the cross for our sins.

God, be with all the missionaries living around the world who are teaching people about you. Keep them safe give them the right words to say. Give me a heart that wants to help missionaries by sharing my money with them, by praying for them, and by sending them things they can use.

God, help me be a missionary to the people around me. I can do this by inviting people to church, praying for them, and helping people who need help. Help me do these things, God, because I want people to know who Jesus is.

Help me not be scared to tell other people about you and Jesus. Help me show other people who Jesus is by the way I act and the way I talk.

In Jesus' name I pray, amen.

Questions:

1. Read Matthew 28:18-20. What are the names of some missionaries you know?

2. Name three things you will do for them this week.

3. Name three people you know who don't know about Jesus or who don't love and obey him.

4. What will you do this week to share Jesus with these people?

Prayer #7: Dependability

Dear God,

Thank you for loving me and for always being God. Thank you for always taking care of us and for promising we can always depend on you.

Please help me be dependable too. Help me keep my promises, to always do my best, and to always tell the truth. God, make me a good helper and a good listener.

I love you and I want you to know you can depend on me to do my best to obey you and to show and tell other people about you whenever I can.

In Jesus' name I pray, amen.

Questions:

1. Read Proverbs 16:3. Why is it important for us to depend on God?

2. How do you know you can depend on your parents?

3. What do you do to show your parents they can depend on you?

4. How can you become more dependable?

Prayer #8: Faith

Dear God,

Thank you for loving us and for never forgetting about us. The Bible is full of reminders that you will never leave us—that you are faithful to us. This makes me happy and thankful.

God, help me have faith in you. Help me believe you can do anything and that you are all powerful. Help me trust you to always take care of me and my family.

God, help me be faithful to you. Help me follow you. Help me obey the words in the Bible. Help me believe your promises and tell others about them. Help me believe you have special plans for my life and give me the faith to follow those plans.

In Jesus' name I pray, amen.

Questions:

1. Read Matthew 17:20. How big or small do you think your faith is?

2. Is there anything in the Bible you have trouble believing? Why?

3. What are some things you can do to have more faith?

Prayer #9: Bullying

Dear God,

Thank you for protecting me and for sending Jesus to die on the cross for our sins. God, you know there are a lot of mean people in this world; people who think it is okay to say and do hurtful things. God, please protect me from these people.

When someone bullies me, help me not be afraid. Help me be strong and not do mean things to get back at them. When someone bullies me help me be brave enough to tell an adult who can help me.

God, give me a kind and caring heart. Help me treat everyone—even people who are different from me the way you want me to. Help me not be a bully. And if I mess up and do something mean, put it in my heart to ask that person to forgive me.

God, I want to be like Jesus.

In Jesus' name I pray, amen.

Questions:

1. Read Matthew 7:12. Is this hard for you to do sometimes? Why or why not?

2. Have you ever been bullied? What did you do?

3. Have you ever been a bully to someone? Have you asked that person to forgive you? If not will you?

Prayer #10: Creativity

Dear God,

Thank you for making the world and all the exciting things in it. Thank you for having a big imagination and for being creative. Thank you for the zebra's stripes, for the colorful fall leaves, and the smell of flowers. Thank you for making each snowflake different and for all the different tastes you give to the food we eat.

Thank you, God, for making each of us different, too. If we were all the same, life would be boring, and you know that would not be fun.

God, help me use my imagination to be creative. Help me use my creativity to serve you. Fill my head with ideas on how I can use the talents you gave me to make you happy and to show other people just how amazing and wonderful you are.

In Jesus' name I pray, amen.

Questions:

1. Read Genesis 1:31. What do you think are the most exciting and creative things God made?

2. How do you like to use your imagination?

3. How do you think you could use your imagination to serve God?

4. How do you think God made you special? OR What are the most special and creative things about you?

Prayer #11: Hospitality

Dear God,

Thank you for sending your son, Jesus to die on the cross for our sins. Thank you for loving us enough to want to spend eternity with us in heaven. Thank you for making heaven.

God, I want to be like you. I want to share my home and my things the way you share yours with us. Please help me be good at making my friends feel welcome when they come to my house. Help me share my toys and other things with my friends.

Help me make new kids at school, at church, and in our neighborhood feel welcome. I pray I will let them know I will be their friend if they want me to be.

In Jesus' name I pray, amen.

Questions:

1. Read 1st Peter 4:9. Do you ever grumble and complain when your friends play with your stuff?

2. If you answered yes to the first question, why do you not like to share?

3. Do you talk to new people at school, church, or in your neighborhood?

4. What else can you do to make people feel welcome when you are around them?

Prayer #12: Kindness

Dear God,

Thank you for loving us and for being so kind and loving to us—even when we don't deserve it.

The Bible tells us we should be kind, too; that we should treat others the way we want to be treated. I don't always do that. Sometimes it is hard—especially when someone does something mean or unkind to me. But I want to. I want to be like you. I want to treat others with kindness, so help me to do that, please. Help me to be kind—not just to people I like, but to everyone.

In Jesus' name I pray, amen.

Questions:

1. Read Ephesians 4:32. When is it hard for you to be kind?

2. When has someone been unkind to you? What did you do?

3. What will you do the next time someone is unkind to you?

Prayer #13: Making decisions

Dear God,

Thank you for deciding to create the world and for deciding to send Jesus to die on the cross for our sins. Thank you for deciding to give me my family because I love them so much.

God, help me make good decisions. Help me make decisions that make you happy and that keep me safe. Help me make decisions that show others how much I love you.

Sometimes it isn't easy to make the right decision, but the Bible tells us how to make the right decisions. Help me remember to use the

Bible to tell me what to do. When I am not sure what to do, I know I can also pray so that you will tell me in my heart what I need to do.

I love you, God, and I am thankful I have decided to follow you.

Questions:

1. Read Proverbs 3:5-6. Do you ask God to help you make the right decisions?

2. When have you made a bad choice or decision? What happened?

3. Do you ask God to help you make good decisions or choices? Why or why not?

4. What is a decision you need to make? Will you ask God to help you or use the Bible to help you?

Prayer #14: Love

Dear God,

Thank you for loving us more than we can imagine. Jesus says the most important thing we can do is to love you, love Jesus, love others, and love ourselves. Help me do that. Help me show love.

Help me love my parents by obeying them. Help me love my brothers and sisters by being nice and not fighting with them. Help me love my friends by being kind and sharing with them. Help me love my teachers by being a good listener. Help me love other people by treating them the way I want to be treated. Help me love you by obeying you and by showing and telling other people about you and about Jesus.

In Jesus' name I pray, amen.

Questions:

1. Read John 3:16 How does it make you feel to know God loves us so much?

2. Who do you have trouble loving? Why?

3. What will you do to show this person love the way God wants us to?

4. How do you show the people you love that you love them?

Prayer #15: Humility

Dear God,

You are the only God there is. You can do anything you want to, but you don't because you are humble. You could even make us obey you, but you don't. You want us to love and obey you because we want to—not because you force us to. So thank you, God, for being so powerful, wise, and caring.

God, help me to be humble too. Help me not be bossy or brag about the things I do and the things I have. Help me use the talents you have given me to show others how wonderful you are. Help me always remember that everything I has comes from you and that I need to share with others the way you share with me.

In Jesus' name I pray, amen.

Questions:

1. Read Psalm 25:9. What do you think the word humble means?

2. What are some things you can do to be humble?

3. Why do you think God wants us to be humble?

Prayer #16: Serving God

Dear God,

Thank you for taking such great care of me and my family. Thank you for all the wonderful things you do for us and God, help me show my thanks by serving and obeying you.

God, you made each of us special and different. You made us this way so that we could all do different things to serve you and show you how much we love you. Help me to use the talents you gave me when you made me to serve you.

Help me serve you in my church. Help me serve you at school by being a good student and being kind to everyone. Help me serve you at home by obeying my parents and by treating everyone in my family with love the way you want me to. Help me serve you by obeying you. Help me serve you by showing my friends who you are.

God, I want to serve you to make you happy.

In Jesus' name I pray, amen.

Questions:

1. Read Joshua 24:15. Do your friends and neighbors know you serve and obey God?

2. What do you do to serve others?

3. What do you do to serve in your church?

4. What talents and abilities did God give you? How will you use them to serve God?

Prayer #17: Worship

Dear God,

I love you and praise you for being God; the creator of the world and everything in it. I praise you for sending Jesus to die on the cross for our sins so that we can go to heaven someday to live with you forever. I praise you for making all the flowers, animals, trees, rocks, water...everything. I praise you for loving me and my family so much that you want us to be with you.

God, I pray that the way I live my life makes you happy. I pray that everything I do shows you how thankful I am for you.

We sing songs to worship and praise you. We listen to people who teach us about you because we want to know you better and worship you. Help me have a heart that wants to worship you with my whole heart.

In Jesus' name I pray, amen.

Questions:

1. Read 2nd Chronicles 7:14. What is your favorite song of worship?

2. What is your favorite Bible story? Why?

3. What are some ways you can worship God when you aren't at church?

4. What do you think is the most amazing thing God made? Why?

Prayer #18: Listening to you

Dear God,

Thank you for everything you do for my family and me. Thank you for loving us enough to want to give us good things and to take such good care of us.

God, thank you for telling us how to pray so we can talk to you.

Thank you for the Bible so we can read about the amazing things you did and so we will know how you want us to live. Reading the Bible is like talking to you and having you talk to us. But I know the Bible isn't the only way you talk to us. You talk to us when we pray, but we have to listen. No, we can't hear your voice, but we can feel you talking to us in our hearts and in our minds. You also talk to us through other people—the way they teach us and help us know you better.

God, help me be a good listener and obey what you tell me. Help me always listen to you because you know what is best all the time.

In Jesus' name I pray, amen.

Questions:

1. Read Psalm 5:3. What do you think this verse means?

2. What is your favorite Bible story? What do you hear God telling you when you hear or read this story?

3. What would you like God to tell you?

4. What are some things God has told you in your heart and in your mind?

Prayer #19: Knowing the Bible

Dear God,

Thank you for the Bible. Thank you for giving it to us so that we can read about many of the wonderful things you have done. Thank you for giving us the Bible so we will know how to obey you. Thank you for giving us the Bible so we can know about Jesus and that he died on the cross for our sins.

God, please help me remember how important it is to read the Bible. Help me understand what I read. Make me a good listener so that I will understand what I hear about the Bible at church.

Help me believe every word of the Bible and tell other people about it so they can believe it too.

In Jesus' name I pray, amen.

Questions:

1. Read 2nd Timothy 3:16. What is the strangest thing you have read or heard about in the Bible?

2. What is your favorite Bible verse? Why?

3. Family challenge: Memorize 2nd Timothy 3:16

Prayer #20 Trust

Dear God,

Thank you for being so powerful that you can be everywhere all the time. Thank you for loving me and my family.

God, help me trust you even though I cannot see you. Help me trust you when I am afraid, when I am sick, and when I am sad. Help me trust you to be with me at school, when I am playing, and when I am away from home.

God, there are lots of bad people in this world and lots of bad things happen. Help me trust you to keep me safe. Most of all, God, I want my heart and mind to always trust you to be the wonderful God you are.

In Jesus' name I pray, amen.

Questions:

1. Read Psalm 56:3. When have you been afraid?

2. Did you trust God to help you when you were afraid?

3. How can you show God you trust him?

Prayer #21: Thankfulness

Dear God,

Thank you for being God. Thank you for sending your son Jesus to die on the cross for our sins. Thank you for taking such good care of my family and me.

God, give me a thankful heart. Help me show my family I am thankful that they love me. Help me show my friends I am thankful they are nice to me. Help me show you how thankful I am for all the things you give me. Help me show my teachers I am thankful I have a place to learn. Help me show you I am thankful for my body eating good foods and getting exercise.

God, we know you give us everything we have so I want to say thank you every day.

In Jesus' name I pray, amen.

Questions:

1. Read Ephesians 5:20. What are you most thankful for?

2. How can you show God you are thankful for the beautiful earth he created?

3. How can you show your family you are thankful for them?

4. How can you show God you are thankful for all he has given you?

Prayer #22: Truth

Dear God,

Thank you for loving me and my family. Thank you for being perfect. I am thankful that everything you say and do is true and that you never lie.

God, help me always tell the truth. Help me be honest. Help me not cheat at school or when I play a game. Help me never take something that isn't mine. Help me do what I say I will do. Help me tell others the truth about who you are and about what Jesus did for us.

In Jesus' name I pray, amen.

Questions:

1. Read John 14:6. Why is following Jesus the only way we can get to heaven?

2. Have you ever told a lie? Why did you do it?

3. Has anyone ever lied to you? How did it make you feel?

4. Why is it important to tell the truth all the time?

Prayer #23: Anger

Dear God,

Thank you for loving me and my family. Thank you for sending Jesus to die on the cross for our sins.

Thank you for forgiving me when I do things I shouldn't. Even though I know it makes you sad and angry, you forgive me and that is a wonderful thing.

God, everyone gets mad or angry. When this happens to me, help me get over it quickly. Help me not do mean things or say mean things when I am angry. Help me not stay mad at my family or friends.

God, when I do things to make people angry, help me say I am sorry.

Help me forgive people who make me angry the way you forgive me.

In Jesus' name I pray, amen.

Questions:

1. Read Ephesians 4:26. What makes you angry?

2. What do you do when you get angry?

3. Are you angry at someone? Will you forgive them?

4. Is someone angry at you right now? What will you do to make things better?

Prayer #24: Grief

Dear God,

Thank you for sending Jesus to die on the cross even though this made you very sad. Thank you for loving me even when I sin and make you sad.

God, when I am sad, please help me trust you to make me feel better. God, I know bad things happen—even when we love and obey you. Help me always trust you to take care of me and do what is best for me.

God, when other people are sad, help me make them feel better by praying for them and by doing things that will make them feel better.

Help me be good at reminding them that you are taking care of them, too.

In Jesus' name I pray, amen.

Questions:

1. Read John 14:1. What makes you sad?

2. What do you do when you are sad?

3. How has God helped you when you have been sad?

4. What can you do to help others when they are sad?

Prayer #25: Health and Safety

Dear God,

Thank you for making us all different and special.

Help me show you how thankful I am by taking good care of my body. Help me eat good foods and exercise. Help me obey my parents so that I will be safe when I play. Help me follow the rules on the playground, at school, and other places so I will be safe.

When I am sick, God, please be with the doctors and nurses who take care of me. Help them take care of my family, too.

God, you take such great care of us so I want to help you by taking

good care of myself.

In Jesus' name I pray, amen.

Questions:

1. Read 1st Corinthians 6:19. What are your favorite healthy foods?

2. What do you do to get exercise?

3. Why do you think God wants us to take care of our bodies?

4. How can you work together as a family to keep each other safe?

Prayer #26: Right vs. Wrong

Dear God,

Thank you for loving us and for giving us the Bible. The Bible teaches us right from wrong. Help me read the Bible and understand it so I will know right from wrong.

God, help me want to do the right thing all the time. Help me say no when I am tempted to do the wrong thing. Help me teach others to do the right thing, too.

God, help me be a good example to my friends by doing the right thing.

In Jesus' name I pray, amen.

Questions:

1. Read Proverbs 2:13. What do your parents do when you do the wrong thing?

2. What do your parents do when you do the right thing?

3. How can you help others do the right thing?

4. What questions do you have about right vs. wrong?

Prayer #27: Our world

Dear God,

Thank you for creating our amazing world. Thank you for having an imagination that could think up things like tropical fish, snow, chocolate, and kiwi. Thank you for making everything different and special and thank you for letting us enjoy it all.

God, help me take care of our world the way you want us to. Help me not litter. Help me treat animals with kindness and respect. Help me appreciate everything you have made and enjoy it the way you want us to.

God, you are so amazing and have given us so much. I love you and I pray you will know how much I love you.

In Jesus' name I pray, amen.

Questions:

1. Read Genesis 1:1 and Psalm 24:1. What can you do to show God how much you appreciate the world he made?

2. What is your favorite thing God made?

3. What are somethings people do that are disrespectful to God and his world?

4. What can you do to correct some of these things?

Prayer #28: Joy

Dear God,

I am so glad you made me and my family. Thank you for loving us enough to send your son Jesus to die for our sins.

God, help me know that having joy in my heart is something I can do no matter what is going on. Help me know that having joy and love in my heart isn't about how much money we have, how many friends we have, or even if we have a nice warm house, food to eat, and clothes to wear. Help me know that joy is not something I can get from things or even other people. Help me know that joy is something in my heart and mind—something that only comes from knowing and loving you.

In Jesus' name I pray, amen.

Questions:

1. Read Nehemiah 8:10. What is the difference between joy and happiness?

2. How can you feel joy even when something sad or bad happens?

3. How can you show other people the joy that comes from knowing and loving God?

Prayer #29: Patience

Dear God,

Thank you for loving me and for being so patient with me. Thank you for loving me enough to send Jesus to save me from my sins.

God, I am thankful you are patient with me as I try to learn more about you. I pray you will be patient with me while I learn to obey you in every way and please be patient with me as I study the Bible and learn to understand it better.

God, I also pray that you will help me be patient. Help me be patient when things don't go my way. Help me be patient when I don't learn something as fast as I want to, when things don't happen when I want them to, and when people don't treat me the way I think they should.

People say that learning to be patient is not easy, but that if we do, our faith will grow. I want to have faith, so help me be patient and faithful.

In Jesus' name I pray, amen.

Question:

1. Read Ecclesiastes 7:8. When do you have a hard time being patient?

2. Why do you think patience helps our faith grow?

3. What can you do to be a more patient person?

Prayer #30: Sensitivity

Dear God,

Thank you for loving me and my family and for caring about what we think. Thank you for being sensitive to my feelings. God you made everyone special and unique and you care about everyone. That is amazing and I praise you for that.

God, help me be sensitive to you. Help me always remember that you have feelings, too. Help me show you how much I care about your feelings by obeying you and telling other people about you.

God, help me be sensitive to my parents and family members. Help me show them I care about their feelings. Help me show my teachers, my friends, and even strangers that their feelings are important, too.

Help me be a good listener and not be rude or impolite.

In Jesus' name I pray, amen.

Questions:

1. Read Ephesians 4:32. How can you show God you are sensitive to his feelings?

2. How do you show your parents and family you are sensitive to their feelings?

3. When have you NOT been sensitive to other people's feelings?

4. When have other people not been sensitive to your feelings? How did it make you feel?

Made in the USA
Monee, IL
23 July 2021